CW01335666

# BIOGRAPH

# INA GARTEN

## Career, Life Accomplishments and Personal Life of Ina Garten

Gail Volner

CopyRight ©

GAIL VOLNER

All Rights Reserved

# TABLE OF CONTENT

# EARLY LIFE AND EDUCATION

Ina Garten was born in Brooklyn, New York, on February 2, 1948. She grew up in Stamford, Connecticut, where she attended public schools and developed a love of cooking from an early age.

Garten's mother was a homemaker, and her father was a doctor. From a young age, Garten was fascinated by food and enjoyed helping her mother in the kitchen. She spent hours reading cookbooks and experimenting with different recipes and was known for her love of hosting dinner parties for her friends and family.

After graduating from high school, Garten attended Syracuse University, where she earned a degree in political science. After college, she began her career as a budget analyst at the White House Office of Management and Budget, working for both Presidents Nixon and Ford.

Garten's government job was challenging and rewarding, but her true passion was always in the kitchen. In 1978, she decided to leave her government job and pursue her dream of owning a specialty food store. She and her husband Jeffrey searched for the perfect location and eventually found a small store called "Barefoot Contessa" in Westhampton Beach, New York.

The store was in disrepair when Garten purchased it, but she saw potential in its charming location and unique name. She spent months renovating and redesigning the store, turning it into a gourmet food shop and catering business. The store quickly gained a devoted following, and Garten's delicious and beautifully presented dishes became well-known throughout the area.

In addition to running the store, Garten developed a successful catering business, including everything from small dinner parties to large events. She became known for her attention to detail and ability to create delicious and sophisticated dishes that impressed even the most discerning palates.

As her business grew, Garten became increasingly interested in writing about food and sharing her recipes with a wider audience. In 1999, she released her first cookbook, The Barefoot Contessa Cookbook, which became a bestseller and established her as a respected culinary expert. The cookbook included a mix of classic recipes and modern twists on traditional dishes and was filled with Garten's signature style and wisdom.

In 2002, Garten's passion for cooking and entertaining was brought to a wider audience with the launch of her cooking show, Barefoot Contessa, on the Food Network. The show featured Garten preparing various dishes in her home kitchen and providing tips and techniques for home cooks. The show quickly became one of the network's most popular programs, and Garten's warm and down-to-earth personality made her a beloved figure among fans.

Over the years, Garten has released several successful cookbooks, including Barefoot Contessa Parties!, Barefoot Contessa Family Style, and Barefoot Contessa: How Easy Is That? She has also been recognized with numerous awards and accolades for her contributions to the culinary world, including the James Beard Foundation's Award for Best Television Program in 2006 and 2010.

# PERSONAL LIFE

Ina Garten is private and has not publicly shared many details about her personal life. However, it is known that she is married to Jeffrey Garten, a business professor at the Yale School of Management. The couple met while they were both students at Syracuse University and have been married since 1968.

Garten and her husband currently reside in East Hampton, New York, in a home that Garten has described as "a dream come true." The couple has no children, but Garten has spoken about how much she enjoys spending time with her nieces and nephews and cooking for them.

Garten is known for her love of entertaining and has often hosted dinner parties and events at her home in the Hamptons. She has said that she loves the process of planning and preparing a menu, setting the table, and welcoming guests into her home.

In addition to her work as a chef and television host, Garten is also known for her charitable work, including her support of organizations that promote healthy eating and cooking skills for children. She has said that she believes in giving back and has used her platform to raise awareness and support for important causes.

Overall, Garten's personal life is largely centered around her love of cooking, entertaining, and supporting charitable causes. She has built a successful career and a happy life with her husband in the Hamptons, and continues to inspire home cooks and professional chefs alike with her delicious recipes and approachable, down-to-earth style.

# CAREER IN GOVERNMENT

In addition to her work as a chef and television host, Garten is also known for her charitable work, including her support of organizations that promote healthy eating and cooking skills for children. She currently resides in East Hampton, New York, with her husband, Jeffrey.

After earning a degree in political science from Syracuse University, Ina Garten began her career as a budget analyst at the White House Office of Management and Budget (OMB) in Washington, D.C. She worked for both Presidents Nixon and Ford during her time at the OMB, analyzing budget proposals and making recommendations to improve efficiency and effectiveness.

Garten spent several years working in government, using her analytical skills and attention to detail to help shape policies and decisions at the highest levels of government. However, despite her successful career, Garten felt a pull towards a different path – one that would allow her to pursue her passion for cooking and entertaining.

She spent the next several years working to transform the store into a gourmet food shop and catering business, using the skills she had developed in the government to manage the store and build a successful business.

Garten's dedication to using fresh, high-quality ingredients and presenting her dishes with beautiful presentation quickly gained the store a devoted following. She began to focus more on catering, eventually expanding her business to include catering for events such as weddings and parties. She also started offering cooking classes at the store, sharing her culinary knowledge and techniques with her customers.

Garten's career in government laid the foundation for her successful transition to the culinary world, providing her with valuable management, budgeting, and decision-making skills that she would later use to build and grow her business.

# TRANSITION TO CULINARY CAREER

Ina Garten's transition from a career in government to a career in the culinary world was a journey that took several years and required a lot of hard work and dedication. After earning a degree in political science from Syracuse University, Garten began her career as a budget analyst at the White House Office of Management and Budget (OMB) in Washington, D.C. She spent several years working in government but ultimately felt a pull toward her passion for cooking and entertaining.

In 1978, Garten left her government job and returned to New York, where she purchased a small specialty food store called "Barefoot Contessa" in Westhampton Beach. She spent the next several years working to transform the store into a gourmet food shop and catering business, using the skills she had developed in the government to manage the store and build a successful business.

Garten's dedication to using fresh, high-quality ingredients and presenting her dishes with beautiful presentation quickly gained the store a devoted following, and she began to focus more on catering, eventually expanding her business to include catering for events such as weddings and parties. She also started offering cooking classes at the store, sharing her culinary knowledge and techniques with her customers.

As the Barefoot Contessa store grew in popularity, Garten began to receive national recognition for her culinary skills. She was featured in various magazines and television shows, and her catering business continued to thrive. In 1999, Garten released her first cookbook, The Barefoot Contessa Cookbook, which became a bestseller and established her as a respected culinary expert.

Garten's transition to a career in the culinary world was not easy, but it allowed her to pursue her passion and share her love of cooking with others. Through hard work, dedication, and a commitment to quality, Garten was able to build a successful business and career as a respected culinary expert.

# ACCOMPLISHMENTS

Ina Garten has achieved numerous accomplishments throughout her career as a chef, author, and television personality. Some of her notable accomplishments include:

- Launching her own cooking show, Barefoot Contessa, on the Food Network in 2002. The show has become one of the network's most popular programs and has remained on the air for over 20 seasons, with Garten's approachable, down-to-earth style and delicious recipes resonating with viewers.

- Winning the James Beard Foundation's Award for Best Television Program in

2006 and 2010 for her work on Barefoot Contessa. The James Beard Foundation is a prestigious organization that recognizes excellence in the culinary world, and these awards are considered a significant honor.

- Releasing several successful cookbooks throughout her career, including The Barefoot Contessa Cookbook, Barefoot Contessa Parties!, Barefoot Contessa Family Style, and Barefoot Contessa: How Easy Is That? These cookbooks have received critical acclaim and have been popular with fans, solidifying Garten's reputation as a respected culinary expert.

- Being recognized for her charitable work, including her support of organizations that promote healthy eating and cooking skills for children. In 2010, she was honored with the Philanthropy Award by the James Beard Foundation for her contributions to the culinary world and her support of charitable causes.

Overall, Garten's accomplishments demonstrate her dedication to her craft, her talent in the kitchen, and her impact on the culinary world. Through her work on Barefoot Contessa, her cookbooks, and her charitable efforts, Garten has contributed significantly to the culinary world and continues to inspire home cooks and professional chefs alike.

Printed in Great Britain
by Amazon

35357316R00020